PARENTING

THROUGH

LOCKDOWN

COMPELLING LETTERS FROM **REAL** PARENTS TO
THEIR CHILDREN

CREATED BY ANOUSKA CASSELLS BY AMORE THERAPY

FIRST EDITION July 2020

Published by Anouska Cassells founder of Amore Therapy – Baby Massage and Relaxation

DEDICATION

I always wake up in the middle of the night with crazy ideas which sweep me away and take me on a journey. This one was different. This one I wanted all the wonderful parents around me to be included. When Coronavirus hit us on March 23rd everyone's world changed. As parents we had our own emotional challenges as well as needing to support our precious little ones. This was super hard as I wanted to capture these wonderful achievements in a book. In a keepsake. To celebrate and remember.

Thank you to all the wonderful parents that have contributed to make this book. All the letters are real and unedited. This is created with authentic words, coming straight from the heart.

You may want to grab a tissue.

INTRODUCTION

We know how crazy the world can be, right? We get swept through the days and years. Our emotions are going through constant changes and sometimes they merge into one. Well not this time.

The Coronavirus in March 2020 forced the UK into Lockdown. This meant everyone had to stay refined to their homes and only leave when completely necessary. Emotions were high and even the strongest of us felt tested.

Before lockdown I was running bespoke baby massage and toddler classes, supporting parents through their early days of parenthood. Providing them with a safe, secure and happy place to escape to. A place to offload any worries. A place to meet new people. A place to smile and be themselves. A place just to be with baby.

This stopped suddenly, on my birthday, on March 17th 2020. I was so upset. For the parents not myself. Where would these new parents find the support they needed? How would they escape and be themselves in a safe and secure space? I needed to do something. I provided online classes and 'Love Bags' to send out to parents to spread a little joy. We shared stories, emotions and had regular question and answer times to ask anything that was on their mind. These parents blew me away. Their resilience was remarkable.

As the days, weeks and months passed I wanted to capture their emotions and celebrate their achievements. This was not an easy parenting ride. They could not pop out when baby was upset. They could not meet their friends for a quick coffee to break up their day. They could not have the grandparents pop by to do the washing up. They were on their own. They were inspirational. Through their help, once again, I have compelled their experiences to create this beautiful book. All the letters are unedited and straight from them. With real emotions and authentic to each one of them.

I am sure you will agree when reading these heart-warming letters that each one of them is an inspiration.

Grab a brew. Grab the tissues. Get comfy. Let's celebrate.

Anouska x

TABLE OF CONTENT

PARENTING THROUGH LOCKDOWN

3rd July 2020

TO MY BABY BOY

So lockdown...it feels the new normal...whatever 'normal' is. You will never remember this, but I'm sure you will read about it and maybe even have lessons about it. It was a time where we should have been out and about, eating, playing, and making friends. Luckily we made some before lockdown started! But we should have been growing with our friends and learning with them. But let's not dwell too much on the negatives.

The positives to come from lockdown were memories, nice weather, and you managing to nap in your cot for a solid hour, if not more!

It was lovely to have your dad off for 6 weeks, he got to see a lot that he wouldn't have normally seen. The weather was great so we went for a lot of walks when we could. Then when he went back to work. So, me and you just had fun in the front room! We did online classes through Zoom and we got to see our friends. You got more and more confident with your food and eating habits. You have learnt to crawl, stand, and move! It has been a blessing to watch.

Things haven't been easy, it's been hard being locked away and unable to go here and there, and I haven't stayed sane and positive through this. I have had my melt downs, e.g. when you've decided a 20 minute nap is ok. Or when you were learning to crawl you'd have me awake for 2 hours 30 mins every night for a week. But that would have happened anyway, and in a way I'm glad it was in lockdown where I could just be resting the next day instead of having a busy day.
I guess I am thankful for lockdown in a way because I got to have you

all to myself. But boy am I excited for a wine with my friends and to send you to Grandmas for numerous sleepovers, go and visit a soft play centre so you can be entertained by anyone other than me for a few hours, and go back to work so I can earn money to take you to all the nice places I promised you.

Anyway, Mum better sign off now so I can put you down for your nap!

Lockdown it's been a pleasure, kind of, but baby boy never forget that whatever happens 'you got this'.
Love from Mummy
Xxx

6th July 2020

MY DARLING DAUGHTER

I need to stop.

I keep thinking about what next. How hard is it going to be to reintroduce you to other people? Your grandparents can't wait to see you but what happens if all you do is cry? Will you ever nap without cuddling me on the sofa? I'll be going back to work soon, how hard will it be for you being left with strangers at nursery? How well will you play with other children when you've had it all your own way?

I need to stop. I need to focus on the now, focus on the positive.

For the last four months we've had daddy home with us. We spent the first month with daddy too, but that passed in a blur. Although he's been working he has had the chance to see you so much more, to see you develop and grow, to get used to your little ways. We've been able to share so much more with him and I know you've loved having him around as well, we've been very lucky.

At least three times a week we speak with granny and grandad (both sets). They've seen you grow and develop as well. Although we haven't been able to see them in person, they've seen you a lot more often than they would have done if it was a "normal" situation. They have spent bath time with you, had food with you and cheered you up when you were grumpy or tired (or when mummy needed a break).

It's been hard not living near family at all, while others might have seen family through windows or in gardens we haven't been able to. There have been times I've really missed having others around, when we've struggled getting you into a sleep routine or found it hard to settle you when you're teething. Fortunately daddy has been great at taking care of you (while mummy goes and has a cup of tea and a cry in peace). Thank goodness friends have encouraged us to get out and meet up with them. And our street has never been so sociable, chatting with people in our gardens or after the weekly clap for carers (they've loved seeing you grow), we even had a photo shoot in our front garden.

Lockdown is now easing. It's time for the three of us to break out of our bubble and reintegrate. But part of me doesn't want to. I love snuggling with you on the sofa when you have your naps. It's been so lovely having you all to ourselves. We're so proud of you though, and do want to show you off to people again, but at our own pace and in our own way.

We've had our first day trip, we went to the zoo and it was wonderful. Your grandparents are being cautious but they will be visiting in the next few weeks, we wanted you to have your home comforts when you see them again. We'll hopefully look at a nursery soon too, I hope you'll be excited, you loved seeing other children when we went to the zoo.

Then we'll be getting on the road. Daddy and I both have September off to spend time with you before you go to nursery. So we'll go and see the rest of the family, go and see your cousins and aunts and uncles. We'll also try to get away on holiday to Wales, introduce you to your first beach and the sea and the places that we love. What fun it will be exploring it all with you.

So I need to stop worrying, but we're going to get moving.
With lots of love
Your Mummy.

6th July 2020

TO MY LITTLE WARRIOR

I am proud of you. You are resilient. You are strong. You are a little heart of fire.

You drive me crazy, you push my buttons, you make me take a cold hard look at myself. I see myself in you.

Lockdown 2020 meant you faced the world alone with no siblings to play with, no parks to climb, no children's chatter. You bore it with a dignity that astounded me.

You taught me as much as I taught you.

I love you to the stars above.

Love, Mama.

5th July 2020

TO MY BABY GIRL

Its July 5th 2020 you are right here next to me fast asleep in mummy's bed. Two days ago we celebrated you're 2nd birthday, we had the best day at Knowsley safari park just you mummy & mama.

You don't know it right now but the world is a little bit crazy at the moment it has been for some months, I'm sure one day you will hear all about the coronavirus and how it brought the world to a standstill. I am so thankful you're too young to know anything about it right now. Mama stopped working and everyone was put on lockdown sometime in March, most people had 1 hour of outdoor activity a day but you're on the shielding scheme so for the first few weeks me & you didn't leave the house at all. We are lucky All our family & friends so far are safe and well.

Before all this started you had just begun some toddler classes which you loved, we had started swimming and we were both starting to make mummy and toddler friends. It was hard for mummy & mama in those first few weeks of lockdown because it had always just been Leelah and mummy but now it was the 3 of us and it was a difficult transition.

I worried about you so much, was you getting enough attention was you getting to much, how was we going to help your development, are you social skills going to suffer? But then something changed and you started to blossom, you started to talk you started to stand up and eventually would walk around holding onto just one hand. Mummy & mama reconnected and we began enjoying our little family. Eventually we started going out for walks, we would pack a picnic and off we went, we had some great adventures! Sometimes we would park up in mamas van get the camping stove out and enjoy a nice cuppa tea or even cook some food. We baked a little, played a lot, there was plenty of tantrums and tears. We missed all our friends and family but quickly learned the new way of seeing everyone. As lockdown eases we have been able to see most of our close ones, we are heading to wales next week to finally see grandma and pop pop who we haven't seen since the start of the year.

My favourite thing about lockdown is that I learnt how much you loved our little family, anytime we would do something weather that be a walk or just your milk feed on the sofa you would always say mummy mama Leelah and that's how you wanted it to be. I'm so proud of you and how you unknowingly helped our family reconnect and find happiness enjoying the simple things.

I love you baby girl.

6ᵗʰ July 2020

DEAR THE THREE OF YOU

Well, I am not too sure where to begin. Lockdown has 100% tested you and tested me. We started off so well. We were energetic and had a really good routine. Mummy tried to work every day to bring money into the house and because it was her passion. Her passion that she had spent so long building up and didn't want a nasty bug to take it away from her.

Working and looking after you three didn't last too long though. We argued and I got upset as you all wouldn't play for an hour. But you are all still little and it wasn't fair on me to expect so much from you. You were all going through emotional upset as well, living in the unknown. Sad that you couldn't see your friends and family. Upset that daddy was still going out to work and worried that he may catch the bug.

We worked together like we always do and came up with a plan to relax a little. What will be will be. I decided to put you before my work and only work one day a week instead of 5. Also, Daddy was in charge for that one day, so you still had the love and support you needed.

You have all been so good. You have been superstars with the home learning. You have gone above and beyond. I honestly can not tell you how proud I am. Cody you did so well motivating yourself to reach personal goals. Even when you felt the school wasn't setting you enough work you jumped straight on to something else. Bèa the teachers were blown away by your work, with awards flying in as well as big positions to be filled when you return. You are my princess.

Bobby, well you definitely came into your own during lockdown. Having your big brother and sister with you every day. You have kept mummy on her toes, with your sense of humour and individuality, oh and smashing the back-door window.

We have enjoyed our walks, adventures, buying the biggest swimming pool we could find, teaching Cassie to swim in reservoir, plus just being together.

I love you all with all my heart. I want you to know that even though mummy is a grump, most of the days, that I am always pushing you in front of tv whilst I finish my work, I love you soooooooooooo much. I want the absolute world for you all. But most of all I want you to be happy. That is one thing I think you are.

Love you forever.

Mum x

6TH July 2020

DEAR MY LITTLE MAN

Lockdown

Oh this will be nice no more just me and you we will have daddy and Ellie too. I don't have to feel guilty now about daddy missing you grow. I don't have to feel guilty about daddy missing your firsts. I don't have to feel guilty about spending all my time with you and not with your big sister, we will all be together. I don't have to feel guilty about not cleaning and not having a perfect house. I'll have help now and I'll be able to get everything done. I don't have to feel guilty about feeling guilty anymore.

But baby now i have new guilt. We are all locked away in the house too scared to leave i don't want you getting poorly. I can't imagine leaving you in hospital alone with this awful virus. And everywhere is closed.
I'm sorry i can't take you to see grandma and nanny.
I'm sorry i can't take you out to meet new babies and make new friends.
I'm sorry i can't take you on the bus or train.
I'm sorry for all the things you have missed these past few months but

I hope I've been enough.

We have laughed we have smiled we have got messy and sat in the garden staring at the trees and sky. We have cried. I hope i have been enough to help you grow.
Balloons
Bubbles
Squashy toys

Rattles
Pasta
Teddies
Mirrors
Bouncing
Dancing
Singing
Shouting
Jumping
Splashing
Cuddles and snuggles all day long.
I hope I've been enough.

7 months old now and for 4 of them months we have been locked down. But you know what?
You are the happiest baby, from the moment you wake up you fill my heart with pride. You have the funniest personality already and you are just beyond gorgeous.

Baby ill carry guilt every day of my life but don't you worry. None of that if because of you. You have made every day bearable, everyday achievable, you have made every day perfect. You've made me realise I AM ENOUGH.
I love you baby to the moon and the stars.

Love mummy
  X

4th July 2020

MY BABY ARTHUR JOHN,

I'm writing this letter to you to tell you about the way the world was in 2020. You won't remember it as you were only 1 year old.

We celebrated your birthday and naming ceremony in style with a big party with all of our family and friends there. It was rainbow themed and you had lots of fun playing with your friends.

A few weeks later the prime minister announced on television that we all had to stay in our houses to stop the spread of a pandemic called Coronavirus. Mummy started to work from home, and Daddy was furloughed so he could take care of you.

Before this you used to go to nursery Monday to Thursday and would only see daddy when you got home for tea and bath time. You only saw daddy 90 minutes a day five days a week. Now suddenly it was you and daddy against the world, playing all day long. You raced cars, you played James Bond secret missions, you learnt how to walk on your own! You learnt how to kick a ball, how to splash in puddles, how to wave, how to high five, how to ride a tricycle, and how to say "Tractor".

We were so privileged to share this time with you. There were hard moments, days were repetitive, your tantrums were frequent as you found your way into toddlerhood and struggled to express your emotions. You loved to do all the dangerous things like raiding the recycling bin, exploring the cupboard under the sink, kicking windows, and climbing up tall things. We had to tell you "No!" a lot. I'm sorry for shouting. I just wanted to keep you safe.

Lots of people weren't as lucky as us. Some people struggled to afford their home, their bills, even food on the table. During this time the plight of Black and Ethnic Minority people was brought to the forefront of attention when a Police Officer in America cruelly murdered a Black man called George Floyd. Racism became a topic that was discussed more, and those that wanted to help took time to educate themselves, stand with people of colour, support black businesses, donate money to causes that helped push for equality, and bring diversity into their children's toys and story time. We did all these things Arthur, we want you to grow up in a fair and tolerant world, where people are not treated differently because of the colour of their skin.

You missed out on things. You stopped going to swimming lessons where you had been doing so well and were so confident. You stopped having playdates with friends, you couldn't attend any parties or go to any museums or aquariums or on any of the fun adventures that mummy had planned for the Fridays she took off work to have a special day with you. It is ok, one day we will do those things again, and it will be even more fun and even more special, as we will remember when we weren't allowed to do them.

You couldn't see your grandparents, you couldn't see your Aunties and Uncle. We called them on videocalls so you wouldn't forget their voices and faces. And when we could see them safely and were allowed, we went to see them, and it was wonderful. We appreciated them so much more, and it was such a luxury to be able to spend time with them. When Daddy and I are older Arthur, and seeing us becomes a chore, try to imagine a world where we can't touch, can't see each other for months. This was our reality and it taught us not to take our parents for granted. I hope you never have to experience it again, but that you heed our advice nonetheless.

As I write this, we have been blessed not to be directly impacted by the pandemic. We have not lost our loved ones or our livelihoods. We are the lucky ones. I hold you closer at night as I feed you, and in those quiet moments where it is just you and I, and you are getting sleepy, I recount how grateful I am for every extra moment we've spent together, for our health, for our privilege, for all that we have. I love you and I hope that you find yourself grown-up in a safe, tolerant world that takes care of the environment around you. Too many people take life for granted Arthur, you must appreciate every single day, reflect on how fortunate you are, and help those less fortunate than yourself.

Mummy xxx

6th July 2020
TO MY GIRLS FROM LOCK DOWN

I can't believe how much you have both grown up in the last 14 weeks (or however long it's been, mummy lost count sorry). Believe me this was easily done, the days and weeks started to amalgamate into one.

We started lock down very confused and slightly scared (mummy more than daddy). I was still working which proved difficult with you both being at home. Daddy didn't really have much work on but he was enjoying the time at home with you also. I hope we explained to you what was happening good enough.

We started very enthusiastic about and thought of things we could do for the duration, we put a plan together to help set our days out so you wasn't just watching TV all day every day, which would have been the easiest option most days. We stocked up on new books, arts and crafts, puzzles and baking products. It got much easier when I didn't have to work anymore and you both loved having us both at home all day every day.

We would go for a daily walk, the walk was the one thing we all really looked forward to it seemed very exciting to be out and slightly away from the house. The walks were my favourite part of the day as it meant I got a slight break from it all. Don't take it personal but you were both a handful.

The house felt very small by late afternoon as we had spent most of the day in each other's company with only a bit of playtime on the front. It's not that I didn't love spending so much time with you it was just any time I had to myself had completely vanished and the longer we were in lock down the more I became dependent on you all being around me constantly.

I tried my best to hold it together, keep you entertained, bake, colour, paint, puzzles, reading etc. Some days I didn't have the energy physically or mentally. I tried so hard to stay positive for you both but I know sometimes I would slip up and I would end up shouting at you for probably to you felt like it was for nothing.

You both became very close in lockdown and seeing your bond develop was truly joyful for me to watch. However the closer you both got the more confident you both became and the harder you got to manage. It was double trouble □.

We had our ups and downs, good days and bad days, I struggled with losing my job and knowing I'm not going to work anymore. However this did have more positive than negative feelings as it meant I was getting to spend time with you both without the guilt that I used to feel every day I worked. It came at a good time I suppose with one of you starting school in September it meant we got the summer together.

Lockdown was made easier once we sorted the garden out, which meant we could enjoy the sunshine in our own safe space. I loved watching you both play outside especially when the padding pool was out.

In all its been an amazing and testing experience, we've had tired tears, frustration tears, but mainly happy tears. You have taught me to slow down, helped me with my anxiety and I really appreciate how lucky I am to have 2 precious, funny, independent, clever, stubborn and loving girls. I love you so much you will never understand how much I need you both.

PARENTING THROUGH LOCKDOWN

Now that lockdown is lifting and as much as I'm in desperate need of a break from the house and you both I am struggling to let go. We're still keeping to ourselves apart from one of you having 3hrs a

morning at preschool. I think I'm slightly in denial of life returning to a new normal. I'm so excited about spending the summer with you both.

Thank you again, I love you with all my heart.

Mummy Xxxx

6th July 2020

MY DARLING BABY GIRL

Only in my dreams could I have wished for such a beautiful soul to brighten up my life like you do.
You are so so loved, so much so my heart hurts.

I knew at 14 that I wanted to be a mummy and I thought 24 would be the right age for me. 24 came and went and before I knew it I was 30. My career was important to me, travelling was my hobby and my friends and family were my world.
Time was pushing on, I had succeeded in life with my own house and nice car and more designer handbags than HarveyNichols but it wasn't enough. I was newly single and free from hurt, deception and manipulation but I found new happiness is alcohol and fitness, I survived on coffee and no sleep, I thought more about others than my broken self. Then my body crashed, my brain couldn't cope and my soul was destroyed. Unbeknown to me that your daddy came to my rescue. He brought the oxygen for my life. We flirted, we laughed and we trusted that happiness was in our future.

We started dating, it was hard. Daddy had skeletons, your daddy had, before we met brought into this world your two handsome brothers and beautiful sister who for reasons beyond my control I have never met.

In the beginning I had daddy all to myself, we went on amazing holidays, ate in really posh restaurants and shopped until our arms hurt. It wasn't enough I wanted a baby, I wanted you.

We tried and tried so hard, our bodies were healthy but they weren't combining correctly. We went to see the doctor who was like a giant, he had massive hands but he was nice. He said he could help to create a new life, he could help to create you. He said I had a heart shaped tummy which he said was because I had so much love to give. Love to give you.

Daddy asked me to marry him; I did not hesitate to say yes. I felt like a princess on our special day and daddy looked so handsome. We celebrated until it was nearly daylight. All our friends and family were with us and we had the best day. A better day was around the corner.

Camping in Australia for our honeymoon was amazing and it was here we made the final preparations to see the nice doctor. It felt unfair that we needed the help but I was prepared to do anything for you.

At the hospital I told daddy I felt funny as though an overwhelming spirit was buried in my body. It was you! God was looking down on us, he could see I was desperately seeking motherhood, a chance to experience love like no other, a chance to protect you, to nurture you and experience life with you.

A week later I saw you on the camera you were no bigger than a five pence piece. The lovely nurse held my hand and said you were there but your heart was still growing. I was sad, I wanted you to be strong, I wanted you to be healthy. I was scared. Daddy said you were a fighter and that you were our little miracle. He kept the faith.
Two weeks later I saw you again and this time you looked like a little toy car. The same lovely nurse smiled and I saw your tiny little heart beating. I cried, daddy squeezed my hand, my life was changed forever and I knew that I loved you more than life itself.

We grew together and mummy worried every day, I imagined what you would look like but all I cared about that you healthy and most of all happy. Life outside mummy is hard, it's dangerous but exciting. I knew I'd breathe my last breath to keep you safe. Every time I saw you my heart grew. You tested mummy by sometimes laying so still I had to keep checking you were there, although some nights it felt like you were having a disco.

Mummy and daddy made our preparations to meet you. On the day I waited anxiously for my turn. It was a long wait but definitely worth it. Daddy had to wear a silly hat and I had to wear horrible long stockings. I listened to take that whilst you were being born but the sound faded away as soon as I saw you, you cried, I cried, daddy cried. My perfect beautiful darling girl. It certainly was the greatest day.

You were poorly, I cried some more. Then you didn't cry, your little tiny perfect body struggled with life outside. You were taken away to get better. Daddy went with you; he held your hand, gave you kisses and never left you.

I was alone, I was lost, my heart ached with love but it was broken at the same time. How could this be happening to us? We had overcome so much, why were we being punished. Was I such a bad person, what had I done wrong to deserve your pain.

We chose your name because we liked it. We thought it suited you. It turns out its French Hebrew meaning is grace, and you share it with a Persian goddess, the goddess of love, healing and fertility. This could not suit you any better my beautiful darling baby girl.

You are a fighter my darling girl. You came through it and after an agonising wait we were reunited. You were sleeping tightly in the nice warm box, tubes everywhere but that didn't matter you were alive.

We had to stay in hospital but that was ok. Our first feed together was magical, daddy was asleep because he had done it all by himself to let mummy heal. I held you so tightly and everything was perfect, I had you, you had me and we had daddy. The love that passed between us was so much more than I imagined, powerful and unbreakable.

21.01.2020, my life was complete.

The love was so strong it made mummy's brain unable to cope but you made it survive. The Dr gave mummy some medicine and my brain was able to work again.

Leaving the hospital I was full of energy and motivation longing to start our future together. It was daunting but we had each other and together we could fight life and all its challenges. We had already endured so much. I loved you so nothing else mattered. Mummy's brain stabilised and her scars healed. They remind mummy of my path to motherhood and the pain didn't compare to the pain I felt in my heart thinking I would lose you.

I watch your heart beating when you are sleep. I touch your face, I cuddle you in my arms, I kiss you at every possible moment. I am the luckiest person in the world. I cannot believe you belong to me, to us. Am I dreaming?

Slowly we began walking around your home town, I introduced you to nature, telling you about the world, promising you I would always be here for you. Daily, our fabulous friend and family were introduced to the beauty that is you. You formed intense relationships with Nanna, Grandad and your big cousin. You have so many people around you who love you for just being you.

Everyone, even strangers commented on how beautiful you are, I knew that already but your beauty beamed through those stunning blue eyes. We attended baby groups and signed up for swimming lessons, we booked days out, holidays and trips to see family far and wide.

Then, out of nowhere came the bug, the germ. The germ that would shape the future, the germ that prevented us from exploring the world. The prime minister told us we had to stay at home. We were trapped in our house, no one could visit not even Nanna and Grandad but daddy stayed at home with us. The house became our safe zone, just you, me and daddy filled with joy. It wasn't so bad, we had so much time together it was the best. I wouldn't have wanted to be anywhere else. Every day I watched you grow, learn new skills and become yourself. We joined online classes, we learned massage, yoga and we learned how to love the little thing in life. It was a very strange time. I was frustrated that I couldn't show you off; show you everything thing we had planned but we had each other and the bond we have was cemented during this time. The germ hurt people, scared people but made people come together. Our Drs, nurses, care workers, emergency services and teachers worked really hard to protect us, to restore some normality. But what is normal? The normal is scary and constricting but we have each other my darling baby girl and that's all that counts.

I am not ready to go back to work yet but you are only six months and I want you exclusively. Work can wait, I am a mummy now and it's the best job ever. It's hard work, testing and emotional but fantastic nonetheless. New and exciting times are upon us, new senses to be tested, new experiences to tackle and together we can and will do it. It's going to be amazing.

I never knew I could love someone as much as I love you. You must never be afraid to ask for help but don't ever doubt that I won't be here to support and guide you. You can confide in me and together we will find a solution, trust in me to make it right. Nothing will ever change how I feel about you. You are my world, my universe and my all. I love you from your big toe to the hair on your head. My beautiful darling baby girl the world is your oyster, be happy, be confident and be you. You will be hurt, you will be let down but you are strong and you will succeed. Don't let anyone ever tell you that you are worth less or let them put you down. Remember Failure isn't a demon it is an education. Embrace life. Money isn't wealth, health and well-being is. Strive for ambition, completeness and love.

I hope one day you will read this and I hope you get the chance to experience motherhood yourself because it is certainly the best thing I have ever done. You are my child, my saviour and my best friend. Don't ever change. I am your mummy, your protector and your forever. I have changed but for the better all because of you.

Love you lots like jelly tots.

Yours always

Mummy and Daddy xxx

6th July 2020

DEAR ERIN RAE

You are our Sunshine!! And as the song goes you make me happy when skies are grey – recently there has been a lot of grey days. But somehow you and Gracie push us through and make everything seem so much brighter.

Lockdown 2020 has stopped our beautiful little world and caused so much heart ache and anxiety. As the streets emptied of people, it appeared that wildlife and nature were flourishing. At the beginning of lockdown I tried to remain positive and imagine all of the long country walks we would enjoy; me, you, Daddy, Gracie and Roscoe. I tried to stay positive that we would all remain healthy and safe throughout. Daddy was going to be home every day and we turned that into a positive that we would never get this time again and that everything that was happening was happening for a good reason. We were going to use lockdown as the perfect excuse to enjoy our beautiful family.

Then me and Daddy got poorly and that ruined all our plans! We stayed in the house, barely getting dressed or even going in the garden. Family and friends dropped our meals off at the door and we did not see anyone. Gracie was the best big sister and did so much for you so me and Daddy could rest – she played with you all day long, making sure you were never bored. Gracie did jobs for me and Daddy and never complained once!! We are so proud of her!!

Even though it's been nice having us all at home all the time I really missed our routine; our time alone at baby groups, our little naps in bed at lunch time - Instead of baby groups we home schooled Gracie, instead of our little naps I did washing or cleaning…then all the positivity was gone!

Positivity turned to guilt. I felt guilty for wanting to be at work more, I felt guilty for wanting Daddy to be to better quicker just so he could go back to work and get from under my feet, I felt guilty for not having time to play with you and worst of all I felt guilty for sending Gracie back to school because I found it hard to be a patient teacher.

In years to come from lockdown I will remember the anxiety, fear, stress, worry and guilt. It feels like parents have been set an impossible task to keep everything together for their family when really all they want to do is curl up and wish all of this away – I have no control on what is going on at the moment, but I can have some control on how I respond. So this is my promise to you; from now on lets choose fun - lets have family film nights were we eat hot dogs and goodies, let's play in the garden till way past your bedtime, let's get all the messy play out, we will learn new things and play more games. Let's lay in bed all together and watch a movie, lets enjoy family cuddles. If you remember lockdown I want all your memories to be happy

Hopefully soon we will find some kind of normality, return to doing the things we love with those that we love. You keep being you and brightening up everyone's day our Erin Rae of Sunshine

You'll never know dear, how much I love you!!

Mummy xx

6th July 2020

MY DARLING GIRL

You were born after a long and difficult delivery on a Tuesday in August. I watched as first your head and then the rest of you emerged. I had spent 9 months wondering what you would look like and as soon as I saw you it made sense that you couldn't have looked any different. I cut the cord and then I waited with trepidation for you to cry as they took you away to warm you and check you over. Thankfully, you were fine. You spent over an hour cuddling Mama on her chest while you held on to my finger with your beautiful hand before I finally got to hold you in my arms for the first time. Unless you have a child of your own you will never know quite how small or precious that little person feels.

Those first few days were hard as Mama recuperated. I went home on my own each night and it almost felt like you belonged to someone else, like I was borrowing you. We bonded while dancing down the hospital corridors as I rocked you to sleep while Mama rested.

I waited nearly 40 years for you - an older dad - and you were worth the wait. Every parent thinks it, but you are an extraordinarily kind, intelligent, beautiful child. You are the nosiest and most inquisitive creature I have ever met. You have a gift of making people smile as your smile and laugh are magical. You have even managed to soften your grandpa and uncles in ways that I never thought possible.

Becoming your dad has been the most fulfilling, but in some ways the most challenging experience of my life. I hope I have taken to it like a duck to water - changing nappies, rocking you to sleep, reading to you and playing with you. However, as someone who suffers from anxiety and has lots of insecurities, it has also seen me agonising over the minutiae of mistakes I made in my life before you came along (nothing terrible, I just set myself high standards), and I constantly worry that I don't deserve you.

I also worry about you coming into the world of Nationalistic governments, Brexit, Climate Change and now Coronavirus. So if I sometimes seem quiet or withdrawn, this is why.
You make me want to be a better person every day. Because you (and your wonderful Mama), deserve the absolute best.

I cannot wait to watch you grow up. To introduce you to chocolate, ice cream and Coca Cola. To share amazing books, films and music with you. To hold your hand, share hugs and have fascinating conversations. Simply to be part of your grand adventure is the greatest honour of my life.

Kocham Cię little one.

All my love, Tata x

6th July 2020

TO MY DARLING PIPPA

Your brother and all of us wished for you so, so hard - and boy, did you come true! You were the missing piece of jigsaw in our now complete family.

Pippa Grace, and my - did you fall from Grace. You are like heaven on earth. The sweetest, kindest child who fills everyone's heart with so much joy.

Like your brother you love with all your heart. You're a kind soul who sees the best in everything and everyone. Please don't let anyone take your kindness for granted my darling.

You're in love with the moon, stars, birds and all of the nature around you. You love all of life's creations. I love to watch how you daydream for hours playing make believe, you are an angel.

Although your only little you have so much personality already and the biggest heart. Keep on spreading the love.

Stay wild moon child.

I love you with all my heart.

Love mummy x

6th July 2020

TO MY WARRIOR HENRY,

I remember so well being pregnant with you, picturing what you'd look like. Imagining brown hair and brown eyes like myself and your Dad. How wrong I was, you were the complete opposite...better! Fair hair and dazzling blue eyes. Wow did we bond in that week we had together in the hospital. My little fighter from day one! I should've known from then that the fight you had put in at birth would mean you'd have a life you would lead full throttle!

I will be honest I used to struggle, struggle seeing the 'perfect mums' with their 'perfectly inline child' that never tiptoed over the 'line' however up until recently I've began to realise that's not you! And you know what...I love you even more for that! You'll always be the child that laughs the loudest, jumps in (every single) puddle on the way home from school, climbs the highest tree, dances like there is no one watching, sings at the top of your lungs. After all life is not a dress rehearsal is it?

I am unbelievably proud of you. You are the sweetest, kindest most thoughtful boy.   You love so hard and with all your heart, keep it that way, never let anyone lead you to believe it should be any other way.

Even in this sometimes cruel world we live in you see the greatness and adventure in everything you do, don't let that change.

Your strong mind will take you so far. Please don't waste it, even if it has given mummy a few (a lot!) of grey hairs. Continue to live your life to the fullest, don't let anyone dampen your sparkle.

Parenting Through Lockdown

I love you with all my heart.

Mummy x

6th July 2020

DEAR VINCENT

I am so grateful to be your mother and to be able to spend so much time with you and your brother during lock down. Gosh was it intense. Some days felt like a triumph, like the ones where the sun shone and the garden was inviting. You learned to stand and walk and dance and talk and I didn't miss a thing! Some days felt like a failure, your needs were great and plentiful and my tried and tested solutions weren't cutting it, forever juggling expectations with reality. Being a mother has been a learning curve of letting go of control. I have come to realise that I am a supporting role to your great story, instrumental in its beginnings and excited to see your future. Any time I doubt my abilities to be the best mum I realise that I need to shift my focus back to you and your story. You are the boss baby. The expert baby. So, in tune with your own needs and amazing at communicating them if only I will listen. Motherhood is not about what people think of me. Or what I think of myself. It's about connecting, listening, It's about you in each individual moment. I hope you feel loved and understood.

To any mums reading this I hope you don't see this as a call for martyrdom. I am only able to give my children what I HAVE. And that means self-care. Self-care. Self-care. If I am grumpy or tearful or just down, I can usually see a link to frustrations from my own unmet needs. I am not that far removed from my past as a baby. I still need to sleep well eat well feel loved and understood. Do not underestimate the power of your own needs and seek out ways to get them satisfied.

A lot of what I value as a mother now has been reinforced by my time spent at sessions with the author of this book. Anouska's classes were a perfect balance between reconnecting with our babies and recharging our own batteries. She is an angel and we miss her.

Love you now and forever,
Mummy

ACKNOWLEDGEDGMENTS

To all the parents, grandparents, aunties and uncles, cousins, friends and strangers who are reading this,

I sincerely hope you have enjoyed reading these heartful letters. These letters of pure emotion which have been thrown to the wind the past few months. As lockdown eases and life returns to the 'new' norm we will be sent on another unknown journey. As we set foot on our new paths please take time to reflect. Take time to remember those close by.

Life can whisk us up in an instant and our lives can be run by our minds and not our hearts. Remember what makes your heart sing. What your unique drive is. What makes you smile. What makes you energetic with passion and love.

Thank you with all my heart,

Anouska x

Parenting Through Lockdown

ABOUT THE AUTHOR

Anouska Cassells is the founder of Amore Therapy – Baby Massage and Relaxation, offering safe and positive classes for new parents to explore their individuality and unique values. She holds a BA Honours in Early Years and Education as well as Sleep Coaching. She also holds endless qualifications in Baby Massage, Baby Yoga, Learn, Stretch and Play, Forest School plus so much more. She has more than eighteen years of experience working with, and managing, Ofsted Outstanding nursery settings. Anouska is passionate about parenthood and child development. Anouska lives in Derbyshire with her husband and three children. I hope you all enjoyed reading these letter as I did.

Printed in Great Britain
by Amazon

43684209R00031